TO HAVE
TO SHOOT IRISHMEN

a play with songs

Lizzie Nunnery

T0333831

To Have to Shoot Irishmen
premiered as an Almanac Arts production
in association with Liverpool Irish Festival and Claire Bigley.

It opened at Omnibus Theatre on 2 October 2018.

TO HAVE TO SHOOT IRISHMEN
a play with songs by Lizzie Nunnery

Frank	Gerard Kearns
Hanna	Elinor Lawless
William	Robbie O'Neill
Vane	Russell Richardson

Director	Gemma Kerr
Set and Costume Designer	Rachael Rooney
Lighting Designer	Richard Owen
Original music by	Vidar Norheim and Lizzie Nunnery
Sound Designer/ Musical Director	Vidar Norheim
Dramaturg	Lindsay Rodden
Assistant Director	Chantell Walker
Associate Producer	Claire Bigley
Assistant Producer	Alex Stringer
Consultant Producer	Amy Fisher
Design Mentor	Katie Scott
Press and PR	Duncan Clarke PR
Graphic Designer	Andy Donovan

To Have to Shoot Irishmen is supported by the Oppenheim-John Downes Memorial Trust.

The script was originally commissioned by Druid.

BIOGRAPHIES

Gerard Kearns | Frank

Gerard played Ian Gallagher in acclaimed TV drama *Shameless* and starred in
the BAFTA Award-winning *The Mark of Cain*, both for Channel 4. His other
credits include *The Smoke* (Sky 1), *The Last Kingdom* (BBC), *Looking for Eric*,
Trespass Against Us and Mike Leigh's forthcoming film *Peterloo* (all Film 4).
His stage work includes *The Accrington Pals* and *Much Ado About Nothing* at
Manchester Royal Exchange, and the West End production of Tim's Firths's *Sign
of the Times*. In 2019 he will be seen in the HBO/Sky miniseries *Chernobyl*.

Elinor Lawless | *Hanna*

Elinor trained at the Bristol Old Vic Theatre School, where she was awarded
the Peter Akerman Award for Best Comedy Actress.

Theatre includes: *The End of Hope* (Soho /Orange Tree); *Bakkhai* (Almeida);
King Charles III (West End); *Stone Cold Murder* (Mill at Sonning); *NewsRevue*
(Canal Theatre Café); *The Roaring Girl* (Shakespeare's Globe); *Much Ado
About Nothing* (Tobacco Factory); *Hamlet* (Red Rose Chain); *All's Well That
Ends Well* (tour); *Next Door's Baby, Twelfth Night* (Orange Tree); and *Success
Story* (Pleasance).

Elinor has also worked as a stand-up comedian, reaching the semi-finals
of *Amused Moose* (Best New Comedy Act) and *Laughing Horse* (Best New
Stand-Up).

Robbie O'Neill | *William*

A former builder, Robbie trained at Bristol Old Vic Theatre school. TV credits
include: *Jonathan Strange and Mr Norrell*, playing the regular role of Lucas
(BBC America); *Casualty* and *Father Brown* (BBC). More recently he played
series regular DC Jones in the award winning ITV drama *Little Boy Blue*
alongside Stephen Graham. On stage, he won critical acclaim for his portrayal
of soldier McKay in *Lines* at The Yard. He's also a talented writer, developing
plays with both the Royal Court and Liverpool Everyman, and is currently
working on his debut short film *Seconds Out*, which he wrote and will appear
in alongside Faye Marsay.

Russell Richardson | *Vane*

Russell trained at East 15 Acting School in London and has been working professionally as an Actor for over 30 years.

Theatre includes: *The Secret Garden* (Theatre by the Lake, Keswick) *Chip Shop Chips* (Box of Tricks); *An August Bank Holiday Lark, The Winter's Tale* (Northern Broadsides); *Pinocchio, The Hobbit, Oliver Twist* (Duke's Playhouse, Lancaster); *Hindle Wakes, A View from the Bridge, Ghosts* (Bolton Octagon); *Our Day Out, Death Trap* (Oldham Coliseum); *The Enough Project* (DepArts/Lowry Theatre); *The Wind in the Willows* (West Yorkshire Playhouse); *Singin' in the Rain* (London Palladium); *Bouncers* (Crescent Theatre, Birmingham); *Pied Piper* (Sherman Theatre, Cardiff); *Midsummer Night's Dream* (Regent's Park Open Air Theatre); *The Miracle Tour* (Everyman Theatre, Cheltenham).

He has also worked extensively in radio and TV drama, including appearances in *Bancroft, Last Tango in Halifax, Creeped Out, Coronation Street, Drop the Dead Donkey, Dalziel and Pascoe* and *Poirot*. Film work includes the BAFTA-nominated *Scent* (Screen Yorkshire).

Lizzie Nunnery | *Playwright*

Co-Artistic Director of Almanac Arts, Lizzie's first play *Intemperance* (Liverpool Everyman) was awarded five stars by the *Guardian* and shortlisted for the Meyer-Whitworth Award. She co-wrote *Unprotected*, winner of the Amnesty International Award for Freedom of Expression (Everyman/Traverse Edinburgh). *The Swallowing Dark* (Liverpool Playhouse Studio, Theatre503, Inis Nua Theatre Philadelphia USA), was shortlisted for the Susan Smith Blackburn Award, as was her play with songs *Narvik* (Box of Tricks UK tour 2017, Nordland Theatre Norwegian tour 2019), which went on to win Best New Play at the UK Theatre Awards. Recent work includes play with songs *The Sum* (Everyman), *The People Are Singing* (Royal Exchange Studio, Manchester), *The Snow Dragons* (National Theatre), and poetry and music piece *Horny Handed Tons of Soil* (Unity Theatre/Phrased & Confused UK tour 2018). She has written extensively for BBC Radio and is also a poet, singer and songwriter, performing with producer/composer Vidar Norheim. Her original feature film *With Love* is in development with Blue Horizon Productions.

Gemma Kerr | *Director*

Gemma is a freelance director and theatre-maker, and Associate Artist of Almanac for whom she directed *Liars* (Cornerstone Theatre, Liverpool). Her directing work includes *Spiked* by Félicité du Jeu (Pleasance), *Macbeth* (Omnibus Clapham); *Clothes Swap Theatre Party* (Derby Theatre), *Scarberia* by Evan Placey (York Theatre Royal). *Airswimming* by Charlotte Jones (Courtyard Theatre); *Hitting Town* by Stephen Poliakoff (Southwark Playhouse). She runs High Hearted Theatre with writer Marcelo dos Santos, creating original work for non-conventional theatre spaces, their productions including: *Lovers Walk* (Brighton Fringe Festival, Southwark Playhouse), *Cheer Up, This Is Only the Beginning* (Liverpool Everyman and Playhouse), *This Place Means* (Greenwich, Docklands International Festival) and *The End of History* (in association with Soho Theatre). Gemma is an Associate Director of Forward Theatre Project and Associate Artist of Omnibus in Clapham.

Rachel Rooney | *Designer*

Rachael studied Art at Central St Martin's School of Art and Design, where she discovered her passion for theatre design. She subsequently worked as a scenic artist and set dresser for an events company, before taking a place on the Design Course at Liverpool Institute for Performing Arts.

LIPA design credits include: *Skriker* by Caryl Churchill; *Road* by Jim Cartwright; *The City and the Value of Things,* working with Young Everyman Playhouse. *To Have to Shoot Irishmen* will be her first professional production. She is an Associate Emerging Artist of Almanac Arts, receiving mentoring from the company.

Richard Owen | *Lighting Designer*

Richard spent eighteen years as a Head of Department with Sheffield Crucible and Manchester Royal Exchange.

Most recent lighting designs: *Narvik* for Box of Tricks, *Flexn Iceland* for Manchester International Festival and Reykjavik Arts Festival, *Country Wife* for Manchester Met University, *Edmund the Learned Pig* for Fitting Multimedia, *Plastic Figurines* for Box of Tricks at Liverpool Playhouse, *Rolling Stone* for Royal Exchange Theatre and West Yorkshire Playhouse, and *Tree* for Daniel Kitson at the Old Vic. Past designs include *The Gatekeeper*, *Winterlong*, *Powder Monkey*, *Salt*, *The Palace of the End* for Royal Exchange Theatre, and *Brassed Off*, *Bouncers*, *Ed*, *Bedevilled* and *The Little Mermaid* for Crucible Theatre, Sheffield.

Vidar Norheim | *Composer and Musician*

Vidar Norheim is a multi-instrumentalist, composer and producer originally from Norway. He studied BA Music at Liverpool Institute for Performing Arts where he now is a visiting lecturer.

Vidar has toured worldwide as a member of Liverpool's alt pop unit Wave Machines and worked extensively in a folk duo with Lizzie Nunnery. In 2011 he was named as Norway's most promising songwriting talent, winning a place at Song: Expo in Trondheim alongside many of the world's leading songwriters and producers. His solo debut EP, *Blind Carbon Copy*, was released in 2016.

His theatre credits as composer and sound designer include: *Narvik* (Box of Tricks/Liverpool Playhouse); *Cheer Up, This is Only the Beginning* (Liverpool Playhouse); *100 Seel Street* (site-specific); *Cartographers* (Theatre by the Lake) *Pages from My Songbook* (Royal Exchange Theatre). In 2014, he performed in *Bright Phoenix,* a play by Jeff Young with music by Martin Heslop (Liverpool Everyman).

Vidar has worked on performance projects with Willy Russell, Tim Firth and Frank Cottrell Boyce. Radio and TV composition credits include: *The Singer*, an afternoon play for BBC Radio 4, and *Monkey Love* for Channel 4. He is currently writing his first film score for the feature film *A World After*.

Lindsay Rodden | *Dramaturg*

Lindsay is a writer and dramaturg, born in Scotland and brought up on Merseyside and in County Donegal, Ireland. She currently lives in North Tyneside, following a year's writer-in-residency at Northumbria University and Live Theatre, where she is developing a new play. She is a member of the Royal Court's Writers' Group North.

Writing includes: *The Story Giant* (Liverpool Everyman, adapted from the book by Brian Patten); *Cartographers* (Theatre by the Lake); *A Modest Proposal* and *Sunday Morning, Dandelion Seeds* (women playwrights' collective Agent 160); *Man with Bicycle, '73* and *Writing in the Dark* (The Miniaturists); *The Almond Tree* (State of Wonder) and numerous collaborations with musicians and other artists.

She has worked as a dramaturg in Ireland and the UK on many plays and productions, especially for Liverpool Everyman and Playhouse, where she worked for eight years. Recent work includes *Bright Phoenix* and *Hope Place* (Everyman); *Scrappers* and *Held* (Playhouse Studio); *Tiergarten* (Metal); *Beyond Belief* (Tmesis/Unity Theatre); and *Narvik* (Box of Tricks).

Claire Bigley | *Associate Producer*

Claire Bigley is a producer, project manager and arts consultant born and based in Liverpool. For fifteen years she worked in Halton, initially as a Community Arts Officer. She was one of the team behind the successful capital build of The Brindley and as Principal Arts Officer programmed the space for ten years.

Claire trained at the Cheshire School of Dance and Drama (1991–93) and went on to study Theatre, Film and Television at the University of Wales, Aberstywyth (BA Hons). It was here that her love of working with artists, venues and people to 'make theatre happen' developed.

She has worked extensively with a variety of companies and artists on long-term development and resilience of their organisations, and how to curate tours, and has worked with venues and companies on audience development and experience.

Producer for the following touring shows: Tmesis Theatre *That's Amore* (2015); *Happy Hour* (2016) and their new show *Beyond Belief* (2018); *Physical Fest* (2015, 2016 and 2017); Whalley Range Allstars *CAKE* (2016 and 2017); Travelled Companions' *5 More Minutes* (2017); *Teatro Pomodoro* (2017 and 2018); *Cabaret from the Shadows* (2017 and 2018); Trans Creative national tour of *You've Changed* (2018).

Almanac Arts would like to thank

Young Everyman Playhouse
Liverpool Institute for Performing Arts
Box of Tricks Theatre
Druid
Studio Theatre Washington

Special thanks to

Cathy Butterworth, Amy Fisher, Victor Merriman, Willy Russell, Matt Rutter, Ashley Shairp and Hannah Tyrrell Pinder

About Almanac Arts

Almanac Arts is a female-led theatre company headed by writer/musician Lizzie Nunnery and writer/dramaturg Lindsay Rodden.

Since 2009 they have worked with some of the most exciting musicians, writers, actors and visual artists across the North West and beyond to create theatre that lights up the senses. Exploring social history and storytelling traditions through live experiments, they challenge artists to blur boundaries between theatre, concert, performance poetry and visual art, making work for gig-goers and theatregoers alike.

For further info visit
www.AlmanacArts.wordpress.com

About Omnibus Theatre

Omnibus Theatre is perched on Clapham Common in South London. Housed in a converted Victorian Library and inspired by the building's literary heritage, the programme focuses on retelling classic tales with a contemporary twist. They are committed to combining art forms, to discovering new artistic vocabularies and providing vital support for emerging artists to create new work within the building.

The team is led by Artistic Director Marie McCarthy. Patrons include Sir Michael Gambon, Matthew Warchus and Sir Richard Eyre.

For further info visit
www.omnibus-clapham.org

LIVERPOOL IRISH FESTIVAL

About Liverpool Irish Festival

Liverpool Irish Festival is an annual event that brings Liverpool and Ireland closer together using arts and culture. It celebrates Ireland's contribution to Liverpool's cultural identity and heritage using performance, participation, entertainment and education in Irish traditions, alongside contemporary music, literature, theatre and art, reflecting their significance in defining Liverpool as a great European city.

The Festival delivers roughly 70 events each year, working with hundreds of Liverpool, Liverpool Irish and Irish artists in a dynamic and eclectic programme that is accessible and affordable to visitors both local, regional and international.

Engaging audiences of around10,000 per year, the Liverpool Irish Festival is proud to receive regular public funding from Liverpool City Council's Cultural Investment Programme, the Irish Government's Department for Foreign Affairs, Trade's Emigrant Support Programme and project contributions from Culture Ireland and Arts Council England. The Liverpool Irish Festival is a limited company (4800736) and registered charity (1100126).

For further info visit:
www.liverpoolirishfestival.com

To Have to Shoot Irishmen

Lizzie Nunnery's first play, *Intemperance* (Liverpool Everyman, 2007) was shortlisted for the Meyer-Whitworth Award. She co-wrote *Unprotected*, winner of the Amnesty International Award for Freedom of Expression (Everyman/ Traverse, Edinburgh, 2006). *The Swallowing Dark* (Liverpool Playhouse Studio/Theatre503, 2011) was shortlisted for the Susan Smith Blackburn Award, as was her play with songs *Narvik* (Box of Tricks, national tour, 2017). Other recent work includes *The Sum* (Liverpool Everyman, 2017) and *The Snow Dragons* (National Theatre, 2017). She has written extensively for BBC Radio and is also a poet, singer and songwriter, performing regularly with producer/composer Vidar Norheim.

also by Lizzie Nunnery from Faber

INTEMPERANCE
NARVIK
THE SUM

LIZZIE NUNNERY

To Have to Shoot Irishmen

a play with songs

FABER & FABER

First published in 2018

by Faber and Faber Limited
74–77 Great Russell Street, London WC1B 3DA

Typeset by Country Setting, Kingsdown, Kent CT14 8ES
Printed in England by CPI Group (UK) Ltd, Croydon CR0 4YY

© Lizzie Nunnery, 2018

The right of Lizzie Nunnery to be identified as author
of this work has been asserted in accordance with Section 77
of the Copyright, Designs and Patents Act 1988

A CIP record for this book is available from the British Library

ISBN 978-0-571-35228-9

2 4 6 8 10 9 7 5 3

For Henrik

With thanks to Declan Conlon, Ger Kelly,
Janet Moran and all the other actors who have
contributed to the development of this play

Special thanks to
Thomas Conway and Brid Brennan

To Have to Shoot Irishmen was first performed at the Omnibus Theatre, Clapham, on 2 October 2018. The cast, in alphabetical order, was as follows:

Frank Gerard Kearns
Hanna Elinor Lawless
William Robbie O'Neill
Vane Russell Richardson

Director Gemma Kerr
Designer Rachael Rooney
Lighting Designer Richard Owen
Original music composed by
    Vidar Norheim and Lizzie Nunnery
Sound design Vidar Norheim
Dramaturgy Lindsay Rodden
Assistant Director Chantell Walker
Associate Producer Claire Bigley
Assistant Producer Alex Stringer

Characters

Frank
(Francis Sheehy-Skeffington)
thirty-seven, Northern Irish

Hanna
(Sheehy-Skeffington)
thirty-eight, from County Cork

Vane
(Sir Francis Fletcher-Vane)
fifty-five, British, RP accent

William
(Lieutenant William Leonard Price Dobbin)
eighteen, Anglo-Irish, from Tipperary

TO HAVE TO SHOOT IRISHMEN

The Set

The set is the wreck of Hanna's living room
following a raid, and it's the wreckage
of the Dublin streets. Furniture and rubble
are piled up like a barricade. On top of this
is an old piano. An area should represent
Frank's cell and the corridor beyond.

Note

Frank's lines in Scene Eight are an edited extract
from 'An Open Letter to Thomas McDonagh'
written by Francis Sheehy-Skeffington and
published in *The Irish Citizen* on 22 May 1915.

SCENE ONE
A ROW IN THE TOWN

Afternoon. Hanna stands in the wreck of her sitting room, looking at the mess.

Hanna (*sung*)
I'll sing you a song of a row in the town
When the green flag went up and the crown rag
   went down
'Twas the neatest and sweetest thing ever you saw
And they played the best game played in Erin go Bragh

So sing of Pearse and his comrades who died
Tom Clarke, MacDonagh, MacDermott, MacBride
And here's to Jim Connolly he gave one hurrah
As he placed the machine guns for Erin go Bragh

Sing, sing of the rebels down at Ringsend
The honour of Ireland to hold and defend
They had no veteran soldiers but volunteers raw
Making wild Mauser music for Erin go Bragh

Vane, Frank and William enter, moving towards her.

A bold English captain was raving that day
Saying, 'Give me one hour and I'll blow them away'
But what was their wrath when those Englishmen saw
All the dead khaki soldiers in Erin go Bragh?

Voices overlap as the others join her singing.

Hanna / Frank / Vane / William (*sung*)
All the dead soldiers in Erin go Bragh
'Twas the sweetest and neatest thing ever you saw

13

All the dead soldiers in Erin go Bragh
Their children will tell how their forefathers saw
All the dead children in Erin go Bragh
Sing me a song
All the dead calling in Erin go Bragh
Won't you sing me a song?
All the dead singing in Erin go Bragh

Rumble of trucks and sounds of gunshots and shouts get closer, louder. This intensifies during the following, joined by sounds of bomb blast, of voices yelling wildly, weeping, calling. Perhaps the other characters move around Hanna, gradually drawing tighter around her.

Hanna Walking. Swallowing dry heat and brick dust. Walking and walking and where is he? Where is he? Nassau Street and Dame Street and Capel Street. Burning in the backs of my eyes, in the soles of my feet. Bomb blasts bellowing from the river, and if he's anywhere he'll be right where the trouble is. Right where no person would want to be – and 'Have you seen him? Have you seen my Frank?' A gang of lads nearly knocking me down, running toward the gunfire. A woman fleeing, dragging a tiny girl and when I try to stop her she sees my 'Votes for Women' badge – cries, 'Jesus, not today! Of all the days?!' Mary Street and Henry Street, turning on to Sackville Street and my God . . . corners blown off . . . windows blown out. A barricade spilling across the way. Flashes of men behind. Terraces hanging open like doll houses; shops and boarding houses turned to fields of broken brick, and where is my city? Where is my city? A noise like a shot – like the loudest gunshot then –

The deafening sound of a shell hitting a building.

The sound . . . the sound as the shell hits, as the side wall of Saxone's slides like water; clouds of dust rising, blinding

14

and 'Where are you? Where are you?' Turning running: Cork Street and Ardee Street and Bishop Street and on and on because I can't go home without you. I can't tell my boy I didn't bring you. Kevin Street and Harcourt Street and Mespil Road and everywhere the crunch of broken glass. Everywhere the air tastes of burning. Corner to doorway to corner. Balling for you, shouting raw. Stumbling on broken chairs and lost shoes. And '*Frank!*' I see you now – in a doorway – hunched so I'm sure you've taken a bullet or broken an ankle. So I run and I tug and turn you. (*Beat.*) An old man looking back at me: an old man I never saw before with skin like crumpled paper, looking up at me with tears on his face. And I follow his gaze to a heap on the ground. And it takes me a moment to understand what it is. A child. Girl of eight or nine with her coat soaked in blood, a bullet through her back. The old fella's looking at me like I might know what it means. Gripping my arm and –

> *Heavy exchange of gunfire in a street nearby. Hanna drops to the ground. All the previous sounds escalate, warping.*

And I know then. Without words I know. I don't know what I know yet, but the weight of it . . . rising, pressing at my chest, my throat. My city, my city, my Frank. *Where are you? Where are you? Where are you?*

> *Sounds and lights intensify. The other characters move away.*

SCENE TWO
A CRIME

Hanna's living room. Afternoon. She stands alone in the wreck of her living room, looking at the mess. She attempts to tidy the floor, picking up broken glass.

Vane stands hovering in the doorway, watching her.
She turns suddenly, sensing him, brandishing a shard of
glass as a weapon.

Vane I did knock . . . Your front door's open.

Hanna It's broken.

He approaches.

Stay there.

Vane My name's Francis.

Hanna Is that a joke?

Vane No. (*Comprehending.*) No. (*Approaching.*) Sir
Francis Vane.

Hanna (*backing away*) Who sent you?

Vane No one.

Hanna What have you come for?

Vane To speak with you.

Hanna To search us? To harass us some more?

Vane *No.*

Hanna Perhaps you should. We're all spies and rebels
here, you must've heard.

Vane I only want to speak with you –

Hanna My boy more or less organised the Rising
himself. Isn't that what you've decided? He's been leading
the men of Dublin in a drill before school each morning.

Vane There's been a terrible run of mishap –

Hanna Mishap? My child's seven years old. He had a
bayonet held between his eyes. His father's missing, then
this –

Vane I know what's happened here; I can't begin to say how sorry –

Hanna You know what they did here? You know what you have to answer for?

Vane I just need a moment of your time . . .

Hanna You see this place? It's been a week – I can't begin to fix it. No one dares come to help us.

Vane Madam, I –

Hanna You see this? Your men?

Vane Not *mine*, Madam.

Hanna They tore my boy's drawings off the walls – a scrawl of an aeroplane – telling me it's seditious. They raided my husband's study –

Vane If I could maybe just sit and . . .

Hanna I won't talk.

Vane I'm not asking you to.

Hanna You could turn this house over ten times I won't give you a drop.

Vane I came to speak with you and nothing more.

Hanna I'll tell you nothing of anyone –

Vane There are things I've learnt this past week that I wish I hadn't –

Hanna You're not the only one.

Vane About your husband, Mrs Sheehy Skeffington.

She looks at him sharply.

I have knowledge of certain sad circumstances of which you should be aware.

Pause. Hanna stares at Vane. He looks at her not knowing how to speak.

My brother's on the front, you know? He thinks it's for Ireland. He can come back here and look at the mess of this and tell me it's for Ireland.

Vane Your husband . . .

Pause as she stares at him. She buckles.

Hanna I know he's dead. Don't come in here telling me he's dead as though it's some great gesture: I know he's dead.

Pause. She leans on the table trying to regain herself.

I walked for three days looking for him. A chaplain on Rathmines dodging my eye and saying he's seen him and he's sure; he's seen him laid out in a barracks morgue and he's certain – and I don't know how he *can* be, never having met him a day in his life, but he's shaking his head and saying it, saying it: he's dead. Is he dead?

Vane nods slowly. Hanna turns to face the wall. She doesn't cry out but physically shakes as she suppresses her grief.

Vane I'd never have let it be – if I'd been there, I swear, I promise you. There's been a crime; I'm here to say that – to say it to you out loud: a crime has occurred, and it shouldn't have been. I'd never have let it.

Pause.

Hanna Did you have to wear the uniform?

Vane I'm sorry?

Hanna *Did you have to wear the bloody uniform?*

As lights shift Frank sings gently from his cell. She looks towards him. He never looks at her.

Frank (*sung*)
The ground is breaking . . .

Shout up, shout out
Hope is waking
Shout up, shout proud
Hearts are quaking
Wide blows the banner

Frank / Hanna (*sung*)
Comrades once scorned
Behold wide morrow
Fearless in faith
Throw off your sorrow
Hearing the call

Shoulder to shoulder
To shoulder to shoulder (*Repeat.*)

Shake off, shake off
Ways that are weary
Take off, take off
Days that are dreary
Hearing the call
Shoulder to shoulder to shoulder to shoulder
Here is the call
Freedom for Ireland and suffrage for all

Lights fade on Hanna. She and Vane remain watching Frank.

SCENE THREE
IN THE END, IN THE QUIET

Around three a.m. Frank shifts about in his cell as he composes his words. William is in the corridor outside the cell. He's hungry and exhausted. Sounds of gunshots and shouts from the streets beyond.

Frank Men and women, it is my duty to make known the horrors I witnessed while in the custody of the British military.

William Quiet.

Frank Throughout my painful time of imprisonment my only comfort was my, my, knowledge that I might later bear witness to the atrocities that, that . . . were carried out . . .

William (*approaching*) You'll be quiet, you hear?

Frank The harrowing proof, the condemnation of a military system wild with, with bloodlust, lost to the so-called 'glories of war' –

William You'll need to be quiet before I'm forced to make you.

Frank I'll need to be talking for the rest of my life: it'll never be said.

William Do it in your head.

Frank Did someone take a message for my wife?

William I wouldn't know. I wouldn't bet on it.

Frank She has no money. There were eight pounds in my inside pocket.

William I wouldn't know.

Frank You're stealing from a child's mouth.

William Nothing much I can do till someone comes to relieve me, and as I've no measure of how long that might be –

Frank Nothing you can do, nothing you can know.

William That's right, nothing *for you*, so no use in caterwauling is there?

Sound of two men, Dickson and MacIntyre, thumping on the inside of the detention room door at the far end of the corridor.

Frank They want feeding.

William Don't we all?

Frank You're hungry then?

William ignores him.

You look like you're hungry.

William What does it matter to you if I'm hungry?

Frank They've had you on the run all day I'll bet. (*Beat.*) Dashed off your feet dawn till dusk and no dinner to show, but still you're planning on just standing there?

William I've a post to keep.

Frank You think we'll turn to rebellious vapour and slip through the spy-hole while you nip out?

William I'm not stupid.

Frank Then what's the fear?

William It's nothing to do with *fear*. Discipline.

Frank Obedience.

William Yeah. A bit of hunger. A bit of fatigue. Discipline. If you lot were properly military trained, you'd know what I was talking about.

Frank You're perfectly trained, I can see that. Trained to stand like a manikin propping up a gun 'cause some fella who's forgotten you said 'stay put' two hours since. If you're hungry –

William I'll be hungry if I want to be hungry and you'll shut your mouth about it.

Frank You tell me what charge is to be brought against me.

William Martial law dictates you'll be held until we're satisfied to release you.

Frank Did they also train you up for that: to spout like the teapot?

William moves away, trying to ignore him. Down the corridor the two men bang louder and shout incoherently. William is noticeably agitated by this.

You tell me what charge or I'll keep asking –

William You should've thought of charges before. 'Fore your lot started running riot all over Dublin, waving your guns.

Frank How many times will you men need to hear it?

William There's a war on in France and you start with this mad shite?

Frank I'm no rebel. I'm no soldier. It's not such a complex theme –

William Listen to Judas now.

Frank Repeat that for me?

William Denying – the minute you're under threat.

Frank Peter.

William Hey?

Frank It was Peter who did the denying. Will you be ill-read as well as obtuse?

William Ah, quiet yourself.

Frank What charge is to be brought against me?

William I've no business with charges.

Frank Your weapon in your hand, half-a-dozen men under lock and key and no business?

William I'm telling you I don't know, so you can stop asking.

Frank You don't know but you could think. You could think to throw out their cloying words and learn some new ones.

William And who would I learn them from? *You?*

Frank I'll tell you one thing more if you'll be polite enough to listen.

William No. No, I won't actually.

Frank If I *was* ever to call myself a soldier; if I was to begin to believe that organised death could bring about a better world, I'd need to be so sure – I'd need proof incontrovertible. I'd need flowers to sprout wherever a body fell, lightning to crack, signs from the sky to demonstrate the sacrifice was just. I'd need to think it and know it and for *me*. Not for my country, not for my army –

William I've no interest in your sermons.

Frank I'm an atheist in point of fact.

William I'm sure you bleeding are!

Beat. The banging down the corridor continues.

Frank I saw a boy shot through the head on the Rathmines road five hours since. Coming out of the church. Rambling along with his pal. Your Captain, *your* man murdered him in the street. Cracked his jaw with a rifle butt, opened his skull with a bullet, left his body in his blood in the road in return for four words like any person's entitled to speak: 'Down with the military.' All it was – (*Louder.*) 'Down with the military.'

Down the corridor Dickson and MacIntyre pick up on this and start shouting 'Down with the military!' thumping louder on their door.

William (*running back and forth*) Hey! Hey! None of that!

Frank I'd like something to eat, please.

Dickson (*off*) Down with the military!

Frank I'd like my human right to eat something.

MacIntyre (*off*) Get me a sandwich!

Frank These men would have their right to sustenance.

MacIntyre (*off*) Pickle on it!

Frank With a pickle on it.

MacIntyre (*off*) A sandwich!

The rowdiness escalates, with Dickson and MacIntyre pounding on the doors.

William I'm not getting anyone a bloody sandwich! (*Beat.*) Someone will come and bring food and allow me to sleep. I can't just walk over the barracks like I'm a big man, just decided to walk over the barracks: there's got to be an *order*.

Quiet falls on the cells. Frank sits down on his bed. Pause.

That's a lie. About that boy.

Beat. Frank is silent, resolute.

That's a dirty Sinn Feiner's lie.

Frank (*pointing in the direction of Dickson and MacIntyre*) Those men are Unionists. Did you know that? The whole of Dublin knows that. It took you lot to bomb them nearly to death and drag them halfway across the city to hunger in a cell on no charges, before they ever once in their lives shouted, 'Down with the military.'

William I don't know about that.

Frank You were just told to stand still and hold a gun.

William I was, yeah, and you might just hold your tongue and let me get on with it.

Pause.

Frank He was round your age, the boy. Half boy, half man, staring down a gun like he couldn't understand a thing about the world –

William Filthy lie.

Frank Bandy like you too. His legs all twisted up behind when he fell. Lay there undignified, his shirt half up his back.

William Shut up. Right?

Frank You never fired on a soul in your life, did you?

William This isn't some kind of forum for your views. I'm not here to get to know you –

Frank You're looking forward to it. Been training up, like boy scouts playing at fighting and suddenly someone tells you the game's on.

William Who's in a game? Hey? Not me.

Frank I thought I'd die tonight. Your Captain took me from this cell and dragged me through the streets, held his pistol to me and debated whether to take my life. I looked at him, looked at his gun, looked at myself from a distance some way above, and I was . . . disappointed. I felt not one grain of courage or heroism and I defy you to say any dying man ever felt any different. (*Beat.*) Loyalty's a funny thing. It doesn't work when you're on your own. And in the end, in the quiet, you always are. You'll act in an army, but you'll answer alone, and not to God. Not him or anyone else. To yourself. And not knowing – not knowing won't save you from a bit of it.

William They told me you were a crank.

Frank That's right, and a crank is a small instrument that makes revolutions.

William I'll bet you get to say that a lot.

William leans forward suddenly, holding his head, then slides down so he's sitting on the floor.

Frank What's the matter?

William Nothing.

Frank Hey?

William Stars coming down in front my eyes.

Frank Not enough oxygen to the brain. Breathe in deep.

William does so.

Big lungful – much as you can. My boy does it. Gets himself over-excited so he forgets to breathe. Have to sit him down and remind him it's in out, in out. Easy as that.

William breathes deeply again and recovers somewhat.

Yeah?

William (*nodding*) Mmmh.

Pause.

There's right though isn't there? There's a right side to be on and if you're not on it you're against it.

Frank And what if almost everyone's wrong?

William There speaks a lonely man.

He shuts his eyes, leaning against the wall.

Frank You better keep on your feet: ward off the sleep.

William Nobody's asleep.

Frank Not yet.

William You'd better pipe down.

Down the corridor Dickson and MacIntyre bang rhythmically on their door.

Frank I'm this minute preparing to become ether and slip away.

William (*closing his eyes*) You'd better keep it down.

Lights down.

SCENE FOUR
CUT UP THE SKY

Frank strikes chords on the piano. Hanna moves through the rubble, exhausted, filthy, searching. She sings. Frank, Vane and William sing with her on the refrains. Vane and William tap rhythms on objects in the rubble.

Hanna (*sung*)
    Cut up the sky and roll back the stone
    Tear up the river to hear the mud moan

Tug parent from child, rip flesh from bone
There'll be no going home in the morning

Pull poets from papers and lovers from beds
Draw teachers from desks, dress them instead
In the strange bright costumes of the brave and
    the dead
There'll be no going home in the morning

Pluck my eyes from their sockets, my heart from
    my chest
Tear up the map book, the Bible, the rest
Look over my shoulder, you'll see nothing left
There'll be no going home in the morning

*Dawn light begins to show all around her. She's been
walking all night.*

Paint me a city in blood and in gold
Light me a path for the true and the bold
My house has been gutted, my hopes have been sold
There'll be no going home, there'll be no going home
(*Repeat.*)

*The others sing with her, voices overlapping to a
climax and then suddenly cutting. The sounds of the
conflict rumble around Hanna. Dawn light covers her
as she stares out.*
    Lights intensify before they fade and change.
    *Frank plays a few notes of a new tune on the piano,
building in to a cheerful arrangement: a drawing-room
song to entertain guests. Lights get warmer as Hanna
sets chairs and table upright, rebuilding her former
home, rewinding time.*

Frank and Hanna's living room. It's evening, the Monday of Easter week.

Frank I couldn't just ignore him.

Hanna You could, Frank, you actually could.

Frank I saw him go down.

Hanna How many of your own've gone down?

Frank If you'd seen him you'd have done the same.

Hanna I wouldn't. I would *not*.

Frank You want all our talk to be only that?

Hanna You risked your life for a British soldier, for God's *sake* –

Frank As neither of us believes in the Lord, I wish you wouldn't bother to take his name in vain.

Hanna cries out in frustration.

I couldn't leave him to bleed to death while I could help.

Hanna You have a child, Frank.

Frank If you'd seen the way he moved and called and no one came . . .

Hanna And if he shoots down five Irishmen tomorrow?

Frank I'll run out and help them too.

Hanna Romance . . . Nonsense . . .

Frank You should see it. Jim Connolly and his lot holding up the Post Office like bank robbers. A hundred people running in a thousand directions –

Hanna They'll be hungry by now.

Frank – and him in the middle waving his arms like a choirmaster. And the *looters* . . .?

Hanna They won't have thought beyond breakfast.

Frank People running barefoot over broken glass to grab a handful of shoelaces. I told Jim this – he'd no interest.

Hanna Perhaps he has other things to think on?

Frank We'll form a civil force. We'll draw up a notice – you and I.

Hanna Have they medicine there? Did you ask him that?

Frank If the police are backing off, we're wheelin' in 'fore the whole city's a moil of crime and indignity.

Hanna Jesus, Frank, who cares about a few smashed windows?

Frank Who *cares*?

Hanna Your friends are under siege – you're talking about shoelaces?

Frank They're no friends of mine. Not in this.

Hanna Last time I saw Jim, you know . . . a week since? I'm coming out of Coughlan's Grocers, he grabs me at the elbow, says, 'If you're interested in developments, I wouldn't go away just now.'

Frank The riddle of it. The drama and play.

Hanna He was promising me something.

Frank He doesn't know what he's promising.

Hanna Maybe he couldn't help it any more? Couldn't think or talk another day.

Frank What is he, a child? An animal?

Hanna Maybe it isn't the will of a man, only the push of the whole lot.

Frank There's no such thing as an intelligent crowd, Hanna, you realise that.

Hanna Don't tell me what I realise.

Frank It's not the right way and you know it.

Hanna They got up this morning and they walked into town . . .

Frank We'll never be *right* this way – you *must* see –

Hanna I didn't starve for two months in Mountjoy Jail, to be told in my home what I know and what I see.

Frank There are bodies in the streets. They've torn us all open like a butcher with a knife and they'll take no responsibility.

Hanna They'll be dead, Frank: that'll be their responsibility.

She turns from him, quickly collecting her coat and bag.

I'm only asking you to think as they must think. To feel it that way –

Frank No, Hanna: thinking and feeling are not the same, they cannot be the same, or we're all at sea.

Hanna I'm only saying –

Frank All awash in a sea of blood –

Hanna I can see it as they do.

Frank You think me a coward? You'd have me striding in front of an army like James Connolly? Would that be a worthy sacrifice? Worth leaving a fatherless child?

She tries to move past him to leave. He catches hold of her.

Hanna They need food. They need medicine. Supplies.

Frank You'll have no part in supporting their madness.

Hanna *You'll not tell me my part in this. You have no right to that.*

She tries to struggle free of him but he holds on to her.

Frank I'm willing to die: I'm willing to die as quick as any of them are willing to kill. There's no freedom without peace; you *know* that.

Pause.

You *know* that.

Hanna And what if peace came after?

Frank Hanna?

Hanna What if it couldn't come first?

Frank I saw a boy waving a green flag on a roof top today. Atop City Hall with a smile on his face as the bullets passed through him. As he turned from gleaming show to *flesh* – to parting *flesh*. On my life . . . Could peace come after? After what? Who will we be?

Hanna They can see us free. They can actually see it. Maybe I talked about it and wanted and worked for it, but maybe I didn't see it.

Pause. He looks at her.

This is who we are, Frank. Not theory or letter writing. This is when we decide who we are.

Frank I know what I am.

Hanna Come with me.

She tries again to pull away from him. Again he keeps hold.

Frank I know what *I* am.

Hanna Did your soldier live? The one you dodged death for?

Frank I don't know. His fellas were dragging him in by the time I got to him.

Hanna Good *Lord* . . .

Frank But I would've helped him. The principle stands. It'll be well reported.

Hanna They'll report you a lunatic, Frank.

Frank I've been called worse.

Hanna They'll call you a traitor.

Frank And what is it *you* call me, Han?

She looks at him closely.

What is it you want to call me?

She pulls free of him roughly, exits the living room. Lights down.

SCENE SIX
THE DREAMING

Hanna climbs over the rubble, hits percussion rhythmically. It rings like a bell.

Frank (*sung*)
   Ye choirs of new Jerusalem
   Your sweetest notes employ
   The Paschal victory to hymn
   In strains of holy joy

Lights shift. Four a.m. William is sitting outside the cell asleep where he ended Scene Three. Frank sings 'Ye Choirs' to himself as he looks out of the window, agitated, restless.

Frank (*sung*)
While we His soldiers praise our King,
His mercy we implore . . .

Bomb blasts are heard distantly. As Frank sings louder William wakes with a jolt, jumps up.

It's okay, you're only in a war.

William Shit. Jesus, did anyone (*see me*)?

Frank Not a soul. We're forgotten.

William I thought you were a godless whatever-it-is?

Frank Can't I enjoy a tune? My mother'd sing it.

William lets out a grunt of frustration, rubbing his face.

What did you dream of?

William Nothing.

Frank New rounds of fire whenever there's a moment's peace, men and women out wailing for their loved ones, every soul in the city haunted as they try for rest and he . . . dreams . . . of nothing.

William spits defiantly.

No thoughts, no words; not a feeling in you.

William I was tired, I slept.

Frank My Hanna'll be up and watching the dark, my boy restless beside her. *You* slumber like a babe.

William (*pulling himself up*) This is your thing, hey? You're a pan-banger?

Frank A what?

William Out in the street making some noise or other over the right to make a noise.

Frank I make more than noise.

William I see you now. All air. No bite.

Frank There are plenty who'd disagree with you.

William You'll shout Ireland out of the Empire, is that the plan?

Frank The once-noble people of this country rolling in the mud worldwide: on the front, in the north, in the Dublin streets, in khaki and in green. You don't think someone needs to *speak*?

William The war'll murder all grudges; that's the word of my father and he's a man to know. At the top they're calling it the Scourer. Settle all scores – wipe the Continent clean, start again.

Frank And we'll all be left dancing in the rubble.

William And what do you propose we do? Let the Prussians rape our wives and children? Better in it than out of it I say.

Frank What's that, a slogan?

William This thing's on. We're in it and where would you be? Shouting on a soapbox? Shaking your stick?

Frank You know nothing about it. Nothing of conviction. Nothing of pain. You barely know discomfort. How can you know fear?

William I'm ready to die.

Frank You can say the words, you can't mean them.

William I'm ready to kill and I'm ready to die.

Frank When your Captain held that gun to my head –
you know what frightened me most? I looked in his eye
and I knew if there was any chance at all to change my
place, I'd have that weapon from him and murder him
in the most brutal way. I felt that and what's worse . . .
I knew I'd enjoy it. I'd have seen his insides on the
ground and enjoyed it.

William (*looking over his shoulder*) Keep your voice
down.

Frank Why should I?

William You want him to come in here and hear that
talk?

Frank I'm telling you, killing'll be easy. But living then –

William What if I'm more of a man than you think I am?

Frank I think you're a man like any other.

William I know my duty. What's more, I feel it in my
skin. (*Pause.*) When all this is done do you not think
you'll feel ashamed? That you couldn't even pick a side?

Frank turns away, staring up towards the window.

Frank Let's be done then. Go nail yourself to the cross
and call it loving something. You can all go fight and fall
for Ireland in all your colours and we'll talk no more
about it.

*Frank slumps forward. His hands shake. He tries to
control the tremors. William watches him, approaches.
Pause.*

William You'll go home you know? You'll be home by morning – all this'll be a rough dream.

Frank We are the dream. We're our own dark reflection now.

William I don't know what that means.

Frank What's your name?

William Dobbin.

Frank Your *name*.

William William.

Frank (*turning to look at him*) You're right, William. We're in it and it's on us and if we talk about it enough it might seem ordinary. Only don't hang on for daybreak. It won't look any different from the night.

William looks at him.

SCENE SEVEN
A CLEAR PATH

All hum, creating a drone, slowly gaining volume. As Hanna sings the others circle, beating percussion on objects in the rubble. Discordant low sounds undercut the melody.

Hanna (*sung*)
    A cold May morn is breaking
    Over Dublin's dreary town
    Sixteen men have fallen
    To the rifles of the crown

    Sixteen men stood quaking
    As they faced the rising day
    But before they faced the rifles
    This is what those men did say

Take away the blood-stained bandage
From off an Irish brow
We fought and bled for Ireland
We will not shirk it now

We've held her in her struggle
In answer to her call
And because we sought to free her
We are placed against a wall

Hanna / Vane / Frank / William (*sung*)
Ned Daly, Heuston, Colbert
MacDonagh and MacBride
MacDermott and the brothers Kent
With Clarke and Plunkett died
Mick Mallin, Pat and Willie Pearse
O'Hanrahan and Ceannt
And last of all James Connolly
This message to them sent

Take away the blood-stained bandage
Take away the morn
Take the rifles smoking
Clear away the dawn
Take our bones and make them dance
Take our corpses all
Take our names and pin them
To a bloodstained wall

*This grows and cuts. Lights shift. Hanna stands
watching Vane, still clutching the shard of glass.*

Hanna Sit.

Vane Madam?

Hanna (*brandishing the glass at him*) *Sit down.*

He does so.

There's nothing here you can use to excuse this. Not a letter or a leaflet. Not a day in our past.

Vane You misunderstand me –

Hanna I don't wish to understand you. You sit, you speak.

Vane What else would I come for?

Hanna Not your official line – not your statement, worked out at the barracks –

Vane I was sent out of the barracks –

Hanna All your worth to me is the facts.

They look at each other.

Vane What precisely . . .?

Hanna Tell me who?

Vane The Captain responsible acted on no order –

Hanna *Who?*

Vane He's not a man I'd call a soldier at all.

Hanna What would you call him?

Vane He isn't one of mine. I wish to God he had been – I'd have discharged him years ago.

Hanna His *name?*

Vane Captain John Bowen-Colthurst. Royal Irish.

She stares at Vane.

Hanna Colthurst?

Vane nods.

Vane I'm afraid he . . . he was amongst those who . . .

Hanna turns away suddenly, struggling not to vomit.

He was entirely rogue in coming here. I believe he meant to find cause . . . After the fact.

Hanna He shot out my windows.

Vane begins to rise. Thinks better of it, sits again.

He touched our things. He held my boy by the chin.

Vane This man has a history. At Mons he killed scores of his own – ploughed them back in to enemy troops. In Aisne he drove his boys into a German trench against all commands: slaughtered them.

Hanna This *man* . . .

Vane He shouldn't have been loose in the military.

Hanna But he was. He *was*.

Vane And we must expose those responsible.

Hanna You knew this? Mons and Aisne and –?

Vane *No*. No, not till after. After your husband's death.

Hanna But he was under your command? At the barracks?

Vane In a sense – he . . . If you'd seen the confusion of regiments –

Hanna Did you speak with him? Do you know him?

Vane I sat with him. A little while. In the mess the night before.

Hanna You sat with him and what? Played cards? Passed the time while my husband was locked up across the way?

Vane I didn't know anything about your husband just then –

Hanna *He* did.

Vane I didn't come here to defend him.

Hanna Did you come to defend yourself?

Vane I couldn't know –

Hanna Did he strike you *then* as a man who should be loose in the army?

Vane If for a second I'd thought –

Hanna What *did* you think?

Vane I barely . . . The details I don't –

Hanna You remember.

Vane He was rambling. Mostly. Mildly abusive for the rest . . . He was afraid. Afraid the rebels were in league with the Prussians and all of Ireland'd soon be ploughed with bullets, England invaded across the Irish sea . . . He talked of cancer. 'Like a man cutting the cancer from his own body.' That's what he said.

Hanna I don't understand.

Vane Nor I, Madam. I told him so. I told him to leave off his duties. I told him to sleep.

Hanna His duties?

Vane I told him he wasn't fit.

Hanna Then how is it he walked out of that room –?

Vane If you'd known the chaos in that place –

Hanna You came here for forgiveness.

Vane *I couldn't have known.* He was talking nonsense. Praying and cursing.

Hanna Praying for what?

Vane God knows. Strength? Hope? What do people usually pray for?

Hanna Strength to do what?

Vane He never mentioned his intentions.

Hanna Did he say Frank's name? You tell me that.

Vane He said, 'Isn't it dreadful to have to shoot Irishmen?'

Hanna And what did you say?

Vane I agreed with him.

She stares at Vane. Her son Owen can be heard singing, off.

Madam, I've been relieved of my duties. They'd've torn the uniform from me in the barracks if they could.

Hanna Because you *failed* in your duties –

Vane Because I insisted on coming here. Because I wouldn't let this matter lie. Because I believe that *is* my duty.

Owen's singing continues. Hanna turns towards the sound.

Hanna He's with the maid. He's waiting for me to make his dinner. How will I tell him his father's dead? How will I tell him that?

Pause.

Did you see him? Frank.

Vane After. Only after. (*Pause.*) When I discovered, I . . . I ordered some men to . . .

She looks at him, demanding.

To dig him up from the yard.

Hanna You saw him?

Vane Madam . . .

Hanna *Please.*

Vane He was . . . small. Covered in sacking – I couldn't see his face but . . . He seemed small like a child or a bird. Hard to explain . . . Like I could've lifted him up and carried him out. (*Beat.*) You have to understand, if I could've put myself between those men – if I could've stopped it. If I could've thought . . . If there'd been time to think on what I felt I . . . I didn't *know*.

Hanna They took his walking stick. From his study. His stick and his 'Votes for Women' badge. Souvenirs. Trophies. They dragged his manuscripts away, pages blowing down the street . . . A life's work.

Vane There's a clear path here, Mrs Skeffington. (*Rising, approaching.*) There's a wrong and a right and a clear way through it.

He tries to take her hand. She backs away, still clutching the shard.

Hanna You know, I attacked a policeman once? Or that's what they called it. Locked me up for it too.

Vane I heard of it.

Hanna He grabbed me from behind, pinned my wrists together and told me if I stepped any closer to a certain politician there'd be nothing he could do to protect me. And when I jabbed my elbow in his belly and kicked and spat and scratched he looked at me incredulous. Bewildered. (*Beat. She looks at Vane.*) Because he was trying to help me, you see? I was the savage and he was my saviour.

Owen's faint singing is heard beyond. Lights down.

SCENE EIGHT
THE GLORY OF ARMS

*Sounds of conflict warp and loop: bomb blasts, gunfire,
trucks, shouts, burning buildings. Frank stands on top of
the barricade, facing away: a silhouette. Hanna approaches
him, trying to see his face, but he remains obscured.
Through the course of his speech sounds of conflict get
louder and more distorted.*

Frank I heard a friend say that the hills of Ireland would
be crimsoned with blood rather than that the partition of
Ireland should be allowed . . . Partition could be defeated
at too dear a price . . . I want to see the age-long fight
against injustice clothe itself in new forms, suited to a new
age . . . the manhood of Ireland no longer hypnotised by
the glamour of the 'glory of arms', no longer blind to the
horrors of organised murder . . . After this war, nothing
can be as it was before . . . all things must be re-examined
. . . Formerly we could only imagine the chaos to which
we were being led by the military spirit. Now we realise
it . . . Can we not conceive . . . a body of men and women
banded together to secure the rights and liberties of the
people of Ireland . . . armed and equipped with the
weapons of intellect and of will that are irresistible? – An
organisation of people prepared to dare all things . . .
prepared to suffer and to die . . . but an organisation that
will not lay it down as a fundamental principle, 'We will
prepare to kill our fellow men?' . . .

*Abstract sounds overwhelm Frank's voice. Hanna
follows Frank as he steps down and moves into the
cell, sitting on the ground. She watches him. Silence.*

SCENE NINE
VOICE IN THE WILDERNESS

Around six in the morning. Light is beginning to show, growing gently as the scene progresses. Frank is sitting with his eyes closed, his hands out before him. William is outside the cell, doing the same. They are playing an imaginary game of chess in the air. Beyond the corridor, men's voices can be heard in low sporadic conversation.

Frank Rook to D 4. (*He moves the imaginary piece.*) You won't come back from that.

William screws up his face, concentrating.

William Pawn to H 3?

Frank (*moving the imaginary piece with his hand*) Right you are. Interesting approach.

William No, I take it back.

Frank You can't take it back, the piece has been moved.

William I only thought about moving it.

Frank Once you've touched the piece –

William How could I bloody touch it?

Frank Queen to E 2. Concentrate.

William squeezes his eyes shut, trying to picture the board. After a moment he gives up, throwing up his hands as if knocking over the board.

William Forget it. It's the stupidest thing I've ever heard.

Frank You're forfeiting?

William I've no clue where we are. I'm certain you don't either.

Frank Your one remaining pawn's at B 3, your queen's in a terribly dangerous position –

William Alright, alright, I'm out. For God's sake . . . the lads round there have cards with naked girls on them: I'm stuck playing imaginary bloody chess with you.

Frank I don't know why I'm to be guarded like a wild beast – penned off alone.

William Detention room's full in any case – there's a dozen or so in there by now.

Frank Do they think I'm a danger?

William I doubt it to look at you.

Beat.

How about imaginary snakes and ladders – more my level?

Frank Chess is my only vice.

William Vice?

Frank Eats up the hours something chronic.

William (*facetious*) Did you never think about getting into whiskey or something like that?

Frank No artificial stimulants.

William None?

Frank None. I keep a clean mind – keep possession of my time. The mind's too precious an object.

William Depends on the mind I suppose.

Frank My boy's getting like myself – begging me to get the board out every spare minute. I tell you, I came into my office once – he was maybe three at the time. He was sat in my chair, barely seeing over the desk, shoving about my chess pieces with his little fists, a look of pure intensity on his tiny brow. (*Beat.*) He hadn't a clue how to play the game but he knew for certain he had to frown while he did it.

William smiles in spite of himself.

William My father was always trying to teach me things, algebra before I could walk, wanting me to be the wonder child. He came out of it a little disappointed.

Frank Is that your knowledge or your assumption?

William He's a Major, you know? It's an embarrassment if his child's not a hero or a prodigy.

Frank My father'd have me stupid or cowardly if only I'd stay home and shut my mouth, stop bringing ruin on myself. 'Heroism's for the dead.' That's his little line. Harping on. I move halfway 'cross the country from him, he harps on by letter. There's no escaping that voice.

William The parent's way. It's how they love us, or so I'm told.

Frank I'll tell you this and you won't believe it: I'm in Mountjoy Prison on the hunger strike. Haven't had a morsel in a week – I'm wasting, aching, feeling my body die as I live in it, desperate for any tender word from home and down at my side they place this note. It's from my father. I turn it over. One sentence: 'You will get yourself into these things, Francis: now I only hope you can get yourself out.'

William laughs loudly.

William Serious?

Frank Serious as I stand before you. Tough as a beggar man's boot.

William What were you in for?

Frank Talking. Sedition. I spoke up in Beresford Place, every Sunday for forty weeks – anti-conscription, anti-war. After the fortieth time of saying it they decided it was worth locking me up for.

William I'm with your father: you should've stayed indoors.

Light is appearing through the window. Frank squints into it. He becomes upset suddenly, biting on his finger. William glances at him.

Something up in there?

Frank shakes his head.

It can't be much longer. A whole night and no charges – they'll be bringing the order soon . . .

Pause. Frank continues to look away.

You'll be skipping home: your boy waiting for you at the door.

Frank You know it's illegal – them holding me like this.

William Martial law –

Frank Martial or not, there's no law to it. I was walking home. I was walking over a bridge, no threat to anyone.

William There was a crowd around you – Lieutenant Morris said so – shouting out your name.

Frank And can't someone call my name?

William You were starting a disturbance, blocking the bridge – all the people gathering about you.

Frank Your Lieutenant heard them shout my name is what happened. He heard my name.

William I wasn't there, so –

Frank I was walking home.

William Only there were men out there firing from the pub and if you were holding up the crowd –

Frank I've been taken hostage and dragged through the streets.

William I don't know about that.

Frank You know it. Of course you know it.

William I know he took you out but –

Frank No, I'm only a lying Sinn Feiner, of course.

William is silent, looking pointedly away from Frank. Pause.

If Colthurst comes back, will you speak? For me? The man's a law of his own.

William He's a Captain –

Frank And if order won't contain him why should it contain you?

William *Lower your voice.*

Frank Why, because you're afraid of him? Because you know he's a danger?

William You know I can't begin to –

Frank Come look me in the eye. Will you speak for me?

William keeps silent, moving out of Frank's view. The voices of other men have become more raucous beyond; laughing, playing cards.

Soldier? (*Beat.*) I'm not asking anything other than your duty.

William This is why I should never have talked to you at all.

49

Frank There's a man amongst you with no regard for the rule and discipline of your military – who mocks every personal and moral code. Surely it's your responsibility –

William You really can talk, I'll give you that. You certainly have a way with that.

Frank Will you be the one to speak? Will you be the one to raise your hand?

William Quiet, you hear? You're under my guard.

Frank The one with the strength of character, of conviction, to see beyond the thin frame of rank and file and engage the heart and mind, or is your army just a tin box with no soul within?

William Enough, yeah? *Enough.*

Pause. The rumble of voices continues beyond.

Frank Sometimes what's needed is a voice in the wilderness. Will you speak for my life?

William looks at him through the small window of the door. They stand parallel. Lights down.

SCENE TEN
AN EXECUTION

Lights up on Hanna. As she sings, the others harmonise on the refrains.

Hanna (*sung*)
Come all ye scholars, saints and bards
Says the grand old dame Britannia
Will ye come and join the Irish Guards
Says the grand old dame Britannia

Oh, don't believe them Sinn Fein lies
Every Mick that for England dies

Will enjoy 'home rule' 'neath the Irish skies
Says the grand old dame Britannia

Ah, what is all the fuss about
Says the grand old dame Britannia
Is it us you're trying to live without?
Says the grand old dame Britannia

First I've got the Hun to quell
And I need my gold for shot and shell
So your hungry hordes can go to hell
Says the grand old dame Britannia

Little Paddy, he's the one
He went to the front and he fired a gun
Well you should have seen them Germans run
Says the grand old dame Britannia

Come all ye scholars, saints and bards
Says the grand old dame Britannia
Will ye come and join the Irish Guards?

*Lights shift as William steps forward as though
summoned. He holds some papers tightly. The others
move towards him, watching, listening.*

William No, Sir. (*Beat.*) No, Sir, I didn't. Aldridge, by
then – Sergeant Aldridge had the keys. He'd asked me for
them . . . (*Beat.*) I didn't – I didn't know him. He wasn't
my regiment. But I saw that he was a Sergeant. And
Colthurst was with him so –

Pause.

I don't know. I can't tell you what I thought at the time,
but reflecting upon it . . . Reflecting upon it, Aldridge
must've assumed – he must've thought Captain Bowen-
Colthurst to be the officer of the guard. (*Beat.*) No, Sir,
he wasn't. (*Beat.*) No, Sir, I myself, at that time . . .
(*Beat.*) Sir, *I* was.

51

Pause. As William speaks, Hanna, Vane and Frank move closer, watching him.

Yes Sir. Yes, Sir. I was aware that I was to keep the keys, but as I'm a Lieutenant . . . Sir, as Colthurst is a Captain . . . (*Beat.*) He walked past me and it was clear he had an objective, so I thought – I assumed he had an order. (*Beat.*) I *would* have spoken with him – (*Beat.*) I *would* have but there was barely a moment – (*Beat.*) Terrible. He looked white as paper. Black-eyed. He was . . . tall. I'd describe him as . . . big. About six and a half feet. Broad. (*Beat.*) No. (*Beat.*) No. (*Beat.*) *I wasn't scared of him.* (*Looking at notes.*) I was in a subordinate position and under the pressure of the moment –

He looks up sharply, contemplating a new question.

Then I . . . I stepped outside. I . . . I was out front, outside the guardroom door. Sergeant Aldridge and Captain Bowen-Colthurst were inside with the prisoners. I was, er . . . (*Beat.*) No. (*Beat.*) No. (*Beat.*) For less than a minute – not even that . . . Just to gather my thoughts – Not even a minute – (*Beat.*) *Then*, Sir. That's when he spoke to me but – (*Beat.*) Captain Bowen-Colthurst. (*Beat.*) He said, 'I am taking these men out of the guardroom, and I am going to shoot them. I think it's the right thing to do.' (*Beat.*) I thought it was madness – that's what I thought. I thought it couldn't be right. (*Beat.*) Yes, Sir. Sir, I wanted to tell him so but he was already away from me and – (*Beat.*) That's what I *did*, Sir. I called to Lieutenant Wilson and sent him over to the orderly room with a message. I told him to speak to Lieutenant Morgan – (*Looking at notes.*) to ascertain if Colthurst had received an order to remove the prisoners. I asked him to ascertain – (*Beat.*) I can't . . . I can't tell you my precise words. (*Beat.*) No. No. (*Beat.*) I don't think I said 'Shoot'. I don't think I said a word like that, like 'Kill'. But I was clear. At least

I believed myself to be so. I told Wilson to run and to be clear.

Pause.

Out in the yard, Sir, by then they'd all gone out back into the yard. And when Lieutenant Wilson came back with the reply it wasn't for me, it was for Colthurst.

Pause.

The reply was: 'If you do this, you do it on your own responsibility.'

Pause.

I don't know. I don't know what he meant . . . I don't know what I *believe* . . . I can't speak for Lieutenant Morgan. I can't say if he knew they'd be killed, Sir. But I believed myself to be clear in communicating what was taking place. (*Beat.*) An execution, Sir.

Pause.

I don't know how long. A minute? There was the sound of all the shots and then . . . The lads were all pushing past me – filing out. I went out back into the yard. I saw the three prisoners on the ground – Mr Dickson and Mr MacIntyre. And I saw that he – that Mr Sheehy-Skeffington was moving. I saw then that he was still moving and I started shouting. That he wasn't dead and that, that . . . He was moving you see . . . So I sent one of the boys – Sir, Sir, Lieutenant Tooley, over for orders. (*Beat.*) Maybe five minutes. I can't . . . I can't say how long it was but I . . . *I had to wait for orders.* (*Beat.*) The order came that I was to shoot again, so I called the lads back in – the, the guard. I stood by four men of my guard and we fired again. We . . . (*Pause.*) He stopped moving then.

Pause. Frank moves closer gradually, watching. William doesn't look at him.

Sir, I did. Sir, I wanted to – (*Beat.*) Sir, I'm *telling you . . .* (*Letting his notes fall.*) I *know* what I did and what I didn't do. Don't come at me like I've something to answer for because I'll answer, *believe me*, and me alone. In the end in the quiet. Isn't that how this works?

Hanna, Frank and Vane begin to hum and beat percussion, slowly growing in intensity.

What do I *believe*? I *believe . . .* we were lost. I believe, Sir, that Captain Bowen-Colthurst had lost himself. I believe that *I* lost myself. I believe . . .

The others sing, overlapping, banging discordant percussion, drowning out his voice.

Frank (*sung*)
Ye choirs of new Jerusalem
Your sweetest notes employ
The Paschal victory to hymn
In strains of holy joy

Frank / Hanna / Vane (*sung, overlapping*)
How Judah's lion burst his chains,
And crushed the serpent's head
And brought with him, brought with him
From death's domains
The long-imprisoned dead

They bang percussion louder and louder, stopping suddenly. Silence. William looks out, lost. Lights down.

SCENE ELEVEN
A SEA OF BLOOD

Hanna and Vane stand eye to eye, Hanna still holding the shard.

Vane I've no hesitation in discrediting those men responsible. You and I –

Hanna You and I?

Vane Thirty years I've been in the military, Madam – and my father, and his father –

Hanna Congratulations.

Vane Let me tell you: confusion breeds brutality –

Hanna Confusion?

Vane – and brutality is catching like measles. The *crime* of this is with those who let chaos reign –

Hanna Chaos and confusion . . .

Vane In that chaos a madman killed three people, your husband among them.

Hanna Don't say 'madman' to me.

Vane Bowen-Colthurst didn't know your husband. He's still of the impression he was shooting down dangerous rebels.

Hanna Call one man mad and save the honour of the rest. Save that man too: they won't shoot him for madness.

Vane We'll stand as one. Cut out the rot.

Hanna What if the rot runs all the way through?

Vane We *will have* an inquiry.

Hanna So everyone can tell the same story.

Vane I should hope so, as long as it's the right one.

Hanna Of errors of procedure, methods run askew, a poor unfortunate madman and a few bad apples who'd protect him –

Vane There's no story to this, Madam, there are facts.

Hanna He was seized from the streets, held on no charge, murdered by a firing squad and buried in the ground, his house raided, his writings stolen. You talk to me about *accidents*?

Vane Colthurst isn't capable of conspiracy.

Hanna A man lives his whole life to make change, to disrupt and to challenge. A man like that does not fade away. He does not wither in a moment of inconsequence.

Vane I see you need to believe that.

Hanna I need truth.

Vane The truth, I'm afraid, will not be bent to fit your means.

Hanna No, only to fit yours.

Vane I saw it for myself. In all that muddle of ranks and regiments, in all that fear and exhaustion, in all that mess no one could stop him.

Hanna *No one cared to stop him.* Isn't that what you *know*? No one cared to save Frank's life. Not any man in that barracks. He wasn't worth that much to them.

Vane If I'd been there –

Hanna *You weren't there.*

Pause.

You know your duty, don't you, Sir Francis? I see exactly where your duty lies.

Vane What of *yours*?

Hanna Excuse me?

Vane Your brother fighting on the front – do you think of him?

Hanna What should I think?

Vane Think of the shame you'd bring him before you tar his entire army.

Hanna I've no duty to the British army.

Vane Endless men and boys each moment marching into death in France. You could live with that betrayal?

Hanna My husband will not be sacrificed.

Vane I came here as no one else would.

Hanna You think coming here washes you clean?

Vane You'd've been living in the dark for the rest of your life if it wasn't for me.

Hanna You think you're any better than the boys who fired bullets into my husband?

Vane We're none of us clean, Madam. Are you higher or holier? The friends *you* keep –

Hanna They tied my friend Jim Connolly to a chair. Life barely left in him, they tied him to a chair and carried him out in front of the firing squad.

Vane I came here in good faith –

Hanna You come with your guns to my city, my country –?

Vane I love this country. It's my mother's country.

Hanna Don't you shoot Irishmen?

Vane *I am an Irishman.* I was born here. I won't see it torn apart for some vainglorious notion of freedom.

Hanna (*striding towards the exit*) Get out of my home.

Vane grabs her, pulls her back.

Vane Some things are worth fighting for, some things are worth killing for.

Hanna He would have despised you. My Frank. He would've abhorred you.

Vane You tell me you don't believe it. You look me in the eye and tell me you don't know it to be true. Or is it only Irish rifles you tolerate?

Hanna I am not your people, Sir Francis. I'm nothing of yours.

Vane I know what you are. I know just what you are.

Pause. She stares at him. He sees suddenly that she's afraid, releases her. She gapes at him, looks beyond him to where Frank is standing turned away.

Madam, I . . .

She stares past him at Frank.

I came here to help you.

Hanna 'A sea of blood'.

Vane There's a right and a wrong to this.

Hanna A sea of . . .

She turns suddenly to look at the room, as if seeing the debris for the first time. She begins picking up pieces of broken glass – hurriedly, urgently, crawling on the floor.

Vane (*holding out his hand*). There's a way back from this.

He tries to pull her up but she shoves him away.

If we speak, if we stand . . . Reason will be restored . . .

She continues to gather the debris, becoming more frantic and compulsive.

(*Taking hold of her.*) Hanna . . .

She struggles as he restrains her, pulls her to him. Her hands are bleeding.

Hanna It won't stop.

Vane Madam?

Hanna *It won't stop.*

Lights dim like the sky darkening overhead. Paint and plaster starts to peel from the ceiling and drift down like snow. Hanna looks up.

SCENE TWELVE
THE WALK

Lights shift. The drift continues from above. All the characters look up at it, all humming. Frank moves to the piano and plays a few notes. As he moves away a great sound rings out – like three or four hands moving over the keys at once.

Hanna Walking, walking. College Street and Fleet Street and Westmoreland. Searching, searching. Searching till the sky turns purple, turns every corpse and crowding figure into you, till my eyes burn your outline on the dark. And you're in the trucks battering by. You're in all the windows of all the buildings. You're just round every corner and behind every barricade. You're every glimpse, every shadow, every spot in the distance and I see you and I see you . . . And you're turned away, and you're turned away, and you're turned away . . .

Frank, Vane and William move closer to Hanna, humming and singing.

Vane / Frank / William (*sung*)
When the green flag went up and the crown flag went down
Was the sweetest and neatest thing ever you saw
Our children will tell what their forefathers saw
Was the sweetest and neatest thing ever you saw
All the dead singing in Erin go Bragh

Voices overlap as the piano score develops, swells. Hanna is in the position where she started in Scene One. She looks out, sings, as though it's all starting again.

Hanna (*sung*)
I'll sing you a song . . .

Sounds cut. Frank turns to look at Hanna. She looks back. Lights down.

End.